Kimberly Brazwell and London Brazwell © 2023 All Rights Reserved. Any reproduction of the KiMISTRY Jotnal in whole or in part is a violation of federal copyright law and is prohibited. KiMISTRY expressly prohibits groups or individuals from integrating the concepts presented in the KiMISTRY Jotnal in any third-party presentations, consultations, products, or services without permission.

JOTNAL BOOK - SUPERNATURALS EDITION
Kimberly Brazwell © 2023 | www.kimistry.net

TABLE OF CONTENTS

REFLECTION PROMPT	JOTNAL SECTION	PAGE #
Welcome		**2**
How to Write in Your Jotnal	Welcome	3
Elemental Levels	Welcome	4
Prompt Categories	Welcome	5
Mood Index	Welcome	6
Back Story		**16**
My Superpower	Back Story	17
Meanwhile	Back Story	18
Level Setting		**20**
Dear Jotnal – Intro	Level Setting	21
My Favorites	Level Setting	22
Wellness: My Circle vs. Me	Level Setting	23
My Future Self	Level Setting	24
Nature vs. Nurture	Level Setting	25
I Must Let Go	Level Setting	26
Gratitude	Level Setting	27
Clarity	Level Setting	28
What's Haunting You	Level Setting	29
Manifesting	Level Setting	30
Grounding		**32**
5-4-3-2-1	Grounding	33
Remember How to Have Fun?	Grounding	34
Healthy Distractions	Grounding	35

TABLE OF CONTENTS

REFLECTION PROMPT	JOTNAL SECTION	PAGE #
Stress Tattle-Tales	Grounding	37
Weigh the Day	Grounding	39
Mood Journaling		**42**
Light Day Journaling	Mood Journaling	44
Meh Day Journaling	Mood Journaling	50
Shadow Day Journaling	Mood Journaling	56
Food Journaling		**62**
What did you eat this week?	Food Journaling	63
Summary Stories		**68**
Reflection & Recap	Summary Stories	69
Quick Check-In	Summary Stories	76
Free Writing		**82**
1-Page Journaling	Free Writing	83
Doodles		**90**
Blank Pages	Doodles	91
Fighting for Me		**94**
How Often Do You Codeswitch?	Fighting for Me	96
Family Manifesto	Fighting for Me	99
Self-Advocacy Manifesto	Fighting for Me	101
4-5-6 Talk Table Activity	Fighting for Me	103
Dear Jotnal - Outro	Fighting for Me	107

"Well, I've been afraid of changin'
'Cause I've built my life around you
But time makes you bolder
Even children get older
And I'm getting older too."

FROM "LANDSLIDE" BY STEVIE NICKS, FLEETWOOD MAC SINGER. SONGWRITER. PRODUCER.

JOTNAL BOOK - SUPERNATURALS EDITION
Kimberly Brazwell © 2023 | www.kimistry.net

WELCOME TO YOUR STORY

The Jotnal is a reflection tool with prompts and activities. It will aid you to privately jot down your thoughts and feelings in a journal or diary format. Hence, a "jotnal". As amazing as you are, you may have noticed maturing isn't as easy as adults make it out to be. There are times when you may feel uncomfortable in your own skin. Sometimes you might not feel human at all. I get it. So now, let's figure out why and what support will help.

Take this time to quickly and regularly reflect on who you are, what you're thinking/feeling and what you need. You've survived 100% of the days before now. Let's get through the next season mindfully and together!

HOW TO WRITE IN YOUR JOTNAL

Have you ever wanted to release your emotions and feelings, but you didn't know where to begin? Sometimes a blank piece of paper, whether for drawing or writing, is rather intimidating. Our feelings can often be so big and consuming, it all is hard to express.

One of the benefits of the Jotnal is you don't have to write some great novel about all of your thoughts. You don't have to get the words right. You don't have to censor yourself. No one is checking for spelling or grammar. These are just questions, prompts and activities all focused on YOU. Use what works; skip what doesn't.

This is your private written space. Let this book be a place where you can tell the truth. Where you can not know all the answers. Where you can just ...be.

JOTNAL BOOK - SUPERNATURALS EDITION
Kimberly Brazwell © 2023 | www.kimistry.net

3

ELEMENTAL LEVELS

LEVEL	DESCRIPTION
THE GARDEN	Welcome to the Jotnal Garden where we set a foundation for our stories to ground the body.
THE RIVER	Welcome to the Jotnal River where we flow through meaningful connection to feed the individual, collective and universal mind.
THE VAPORS	Welcome to the Jotnal Vapors where we ascend into deeper resources and information to elevate the spirit.
THE COSMOS	Welcome to the Jotnal Cosmos where we expand our reflection and evolution of self with no limits or boundaries.

PROMPT CATEGORIES

SYMBOL	PROMPT	WHEN TO USE IT
	LIGHT DAY, GRATITUDE AND MANIFESTING	For good days, remembering what you're thankful for and listing your dreams and desires
	MEH DAY AND PROS & CONS	For "just ok" days when you feel mid or blah and you could benefit from weighing the ups & downs
	HEAVY DAY AND 5-4-3-2-1	For not-so-great days and ways to calm yourself down when you get nervous, anxious or angry
	HELP ME	For writing down who your support system includes and why they are your favorite people
	SELF CARE	For times when you need to give yourself extra doses of attention, support and love
	FOOD LOG	For reminders on what you ate, drank, medicine you took, etc.
	REFLECTION & RECAP	For quick recaps, reflections and reviews of the week plus plans for the week ahead
	QUICK CHECK-IN	For a speedy survey of the day and a quick moment of intention for tomorrow

MOOD INDEX

SYMBOL	MOOD	ENERGETIC VIBE
	FAIRY	"I feel empty but I look beautiful."
	IMP	"I feel mischievous and energetic."
	SHAPESHIFTER	"I feel uncomfortable unless I change to match others."
	INDIGO	"I feel everyone and everything."
	WITCH	"I feel powerful in my connection to the elements."
	GHOST	"I feel invisible to most people."
	VAMPIRE	"I feel lifeless unless I feed off the energy of others."
	ZOMBIE	"I feel stuck between being alive and lifeless."

JOTNAL BOOK - SUPERNATURALS EDITION
Kimberly Brazwell © 2023 | www.kimistry.net

SUPERNATURAL VIBES: WHICH MOOD ARE YOU?

FAIRY
"I feel empty but I look beautiful"

EXPERIENCES	Loneliness
NIGHTMARE	Never escaping emptiness
DREAM	• Acceptance • Deeper connection • Meaning
LIVES IN	The Vapors
POWER	Attraction and comfort

SUPERNATURAL VIBES: WHICH MOOD ARE YOU?

IMP
"I feel mischievous and energetic"

EXPERIENCES	Playfulness
NIGHTMARE	Inability to avoid negativity
DREAM	- Joking - Easy living - Light-heartedness
LIVES IN	The Cosmos
POWER	Positivity and levity

SUPERNATURAL VIBES: WHICH MOOD ARE YOU?

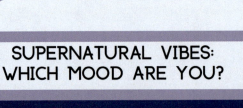

SHAPESHIFTER
"I feel uncomfortable unless I change to match others"

EXPEREINCES	Internal discomfort
NIGHTMARE	Loss of personal identity
DREAM	• Survival • Authenticity • Stability
LIVES IN	The Garden
POWER	Imitation and emulation

SUPERNATURAL VIBES: WHICH MOOD ARE YOU?

INDIGO
"I feel everyone and everything"

EXPERIENCES	Overstimulation
NIGHTMARE	Inability to stop others from suffering
DREAM	• Universal love • Peace • Goodwill
LIVES IN	The Cosmos
POWER	Empathy

JOTNAL BOOK - SUPERNATURALS EDITION
Kimberly Brazwell © 2023 | www.kimistry.net

SUPERNATURAL VIBES: WHICH MOOD ARE YOU?

WITCH
"I feel powerful in my connection to the elements"

EXPERIENCES	Detachment
NIGHTMARE	Trapped in regularity and others' reality
DREAM	• Influence • Autonomy • Power and control
LIVES IN	The River
POWER	Self-assurance and groundedness

JOTNAL BOOK - SUPERNATURALS EDITION
Kimberly Brazwell © 2023 | www.kimistry.net

SUPERNATURAL VIBES: WHICH MOOD ARE YOU?

GHOST
"I feel invisible to most people"

EXPERIENCES	Numbness
NIGHTMARE	Being trapped in others' expectations
DREAM	- Exist without attention - Avoid spotlight - Escape from fitting in - Invisibility
LIVES IN	The Vapors
POWER	Hiding in plain sight

SUPERNATURAL VIBES: WHICH MOOD ARE YOU?

VAMPIRE
"I feel lifeless unless I feed off the energy of others"

EXPERIENCES	Longingness
NIGHTMARE	Never really being alive
DREAM	- Vitality and liveliness - Feel fulfilled - Independence
LIVES IN	The Garden
POWER	Allure and charm

SUPERNATURAL VIBES: WHICH MOOD ARE YOU?

ZOMBIE
"I feel stuck between being alive and lifeless"

EXPERIENCES	Lethargic
NIGHTMARE	Forever stuck in the middle of life and death
DREAM	- Peace - Feeling alive - Not having to fight
LIVES IN	The Garden
POWER	Strength and endurance

MY BACK STORY

Now that we have established some moods, vibes and avatars for you to tap into to understand how you're feeling right now, let's pause for a moment. Every person, situation and character has a creation story. The instance where "it" all began.

- What happened?
- How did I get here?
- What changed?
- When did this new normal begin?

There is a reason why we think, feel and behave in certain ways. In reflecting on what these "supernatural" moods feel like in your life, there is a high likelihood that the back story will reveal your strengths and weaknesses. Use the next few pages to write out your possible back story.

MY SUPERPOWER

ITS FORMS E.G. X-RAY VISION, FLYING AND INDESTRUCTIBILITY	
ITS WEAKNESS E.G. KRYPTONITE FOR SUPERMAN	
MY SIDEKICK E.G. ROBIN FOR BATMAN	
MY NEMESIS E.G. JOKER FOR BATMAN	
ITS ORIGIN E.G. SPIDERMAN WAS BITTEN BY A SPIDER	
MY ALTER EGO E.G. BRUCE WAYNE FOR BATMAN	
MY POWER FLAW E.G. AANG THE LAST AIRBENDER RETREATS WHEN AFRAID	
POWER PERSONALITY E.G. WOLVERINE IS MESSY AND A JERK	
THEME SONG E.G. SAILOR MOON THEME SONG	

JOTNAL BOOK - SUPERNATURALS EDITION
Kimberly Brazwell © 2023 | www.kimistry.net

MEANWHILE...

You may very well be in a shifting season. There will be many more to come in your life. This transition (or shifting) in your life and story is usually an indicator that something - namely YOU - are changing. You are likely not who you were, but not yet who you're going to be.

LEVEL-SETTING

As we begin our Jotnal journey together, it may help (when looking back at this moment in time) to see what your energetic realities and truths were. The further you go on your self-discovery, the more you will see your areas of consistency, change and growth. These first pages may also give you insight in revealing the specific work you might like to do on and inside yourself.

The following pages can either be one-time entries to capture your "right now" thoughts. You could also make copies of these pages and use them for repeated future journaling and reflection exercises. The more you understand how you feel, the better capable you'll be of knowing and articulating (who and) what you need.

DATE _____

DEAR JOTNAL,

THIS IS HOW
OUR STORY BEGINS...

_____

_____

_____

_____

_____

_____

_____

_____

_____

_____

_____

_____

_____

_____

_____

_____

MY FAVORITES

Below, write down your favorite five people in the world in this moment of your life and then think about how or why you best enjoy them. What are the specific things you love and admire about your favorite five? And have you told them lately?

RANK	NAME AND WHY THEY'RE IN MY TOP FIVE
1	
2	
3	
4	
5	

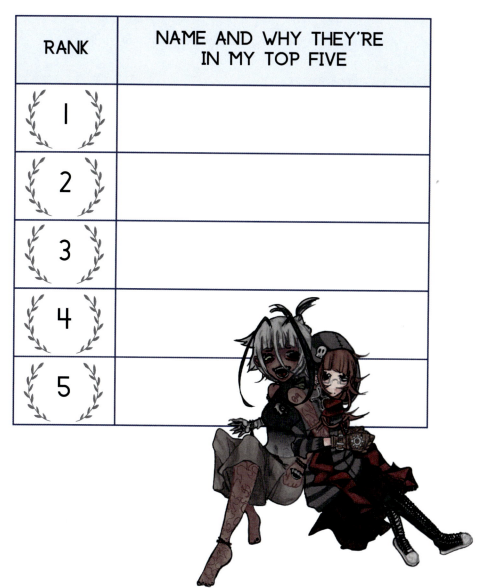

WELLNESS:
MY CIRCLE VS. ME

In the space below, reflect on the 8 Dimensions of Wellness.
How are the people around you doing in each category?
How are you doing in each category?
Are you okay, overstimulated or overwhelmed right now?

8 DIMENSIONS OF WELLNESS	"THEM"	ME
SOCIAL (Support Circle)	☆☆☆☆☆	☆☆☆☆☆
EMOTIONAL (Coping Strategies)	☆☆☆☆☆	☆☆☆☆☆
OCCUPATIONAL (Work Fulfillment)	☆☆☆☆☆	☆☆☆☆☆
FINANCIAL (Income Satisfaction)	☆☆☆☆☆	☆☆☆☆☆
INTELLECTUAL (Creative Fulfillment)	☆☆☆☆☆	☆☆☆☆☆
SPIRITUAL (Feeling of Purpose)	☆☆☆☆☆	☆☆☆☆☆
ENVIRONMENTAL (Community Connection)	☆☆☆☆☆	☆☆☆☆☆
PHYSICAL (Body Health)	☆☆☆☆☆	☆☆☆☆☆

MY FUTURE SELF..

PREFERS TO BE CALLED	
SAYS / DOES	
FEELS LIKE	
FEARS	
IS THREATENED BY	
NEEDS	
IS POWERFUL IF AND/OR WHEN	
DESERVES THIS ONE WORD	

NATURE VS. NURTURE

Your environmental conditions have so much to do with your mood, your energy and how you show up in spaces. When people, places, things and ideas around you feel toxic, what does that bring out of you? Conversely, when you are around people who love you, in places that feel good and when you do things that affirm you, how do you show up then?

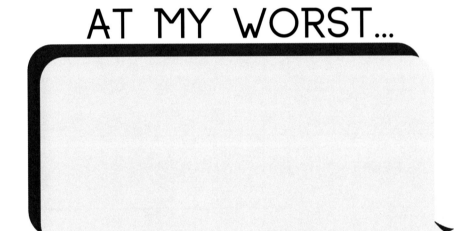

AT MY WORST...

AT MY BEST...

I MUST LET GO... DATE _____

When we're in heavier moods, sometimes those moods are negatively impacted when we hold on to the stress, trauma and the energy of people and things that didn't start with us or don't involve us. Who or what might you need to "let go" of to make your mood a little lighter?

_____

_____

_____

_____

_____

_____

_____

_____

_____

_____

_____

_____

_____

_____

_____

_____

GRATITUDE

TODAY I'M GRATEFUL FOR...   DATE:

TODAY I'M GRATEFUL FOR...   DATE:

TODAY I'M GRATEFUL FOR...   DATE:

CLARITY

I NOTICE OR CAN NOW SEE CLEARLY THAT…	DATE:

I NOTICE OR CAN NOW SEE CLEARLY THAT…	DATE:

WHAT'S HAUNTING YOU?

Without overthinking, list all the tasks in your life at this exact moment. Anything (or anyone) you feel responsible for, write it down. Anything (or anyone) nagging you on your to-do list (whether it gets done or not), write it down. Then reflect on if each item is <u>truly</u> yours.

MANIFESTING

Did you know the word Abracadabra literally means, "I will create as I speak"? If you had the power to write or say something and make it come true, what thought would you bring to life?

_____
_____
_____
_____
_____
_____
_____
_____
_____
_____
_____
_____

GROUNDING

The next series of pages provide reflection tools that will help when you feel dysregulated or ungrounded. Dysregulation is when our energy is flowing chaotically or jaggedly instead of smoothly. Imagine there has been a terrible storm and power lines have fallen over. Envision a live power wire - raw energy - threatening the safety of others.

The work of an electrician is to repair and ground live wires. To protect oneself and others from injury or death, live wires (or ungrounded energy) must carefully be reconnected and channeled back into the ground. When the storms of life disrupt our peace and contentment, it is our responsibility to regulate our safety - and the safety of others - by smoothly plugging back in to our bodies, minds and spirits. Grounding should precede deeper work.

5-4-3-2-1

5 THINGS I CAN SEE...

_____
_____
_____
_____
_____

4 THINGS I CAN FEEL...

_____
_____
_____
_____

3 THINGS I CAN HEAR...

_____
_____
_____

2 THINGS I CAN SMELL...

_____
_____

1 THING I CAN TASTE...

_____

REMEMBER HOW TO HAVE FUN?

In the space below, circle 5—10 ways you used to play when you were a little younger. Have you tried any of these lately? I'll bet they'd still make you smile!

BOARD GAMES	PHYSICAL ACTIVITIES	DOLLS / ACTION FIGURES
MAKING OR ENJOYING MUSIC	DANCING	PLAYGROUND
GAMES WITH FRIENDS	WATCHING TV	TEAM SPORTS
VIDEO GAMES	SHOPPING	WRITING
DRAWING	COLORING AND CRAFTS	PUZZLES
READING	SINGING	DAYDREAMING
ACTING	NATURE ACTIVITIES	OTHER

JOTNAL BOOK - SUPERNATURALS EDITION
Kimberly Brazwell © 2023 | www.kimistry.net

HEALTHY DISTRACTIONS

Feeling STUCK can be stressful and feed anxiety. Sometimes relief comes in the form of changing the routine, pattern or scenery. Think about a time when doing something different (e.g., going over a friend's house, watching a movie, etc.) helped snap you out of your "stinkin' thinkin'".

IDEAS	THE NEXT TIME I FEEL STUCK, I COULD GO / DO...
1	
2	
3	
4	
5	

STRESS TATTLE-TALES

When you're stressed out, you can't be your best for anyone including you. We don't want that. So take a time out and gauge where you are with the common stress symptoms. If you have too many "got it's", drop this Jotnal and go get some help ASAP!

STRESS SYMPTOM	GOT IT?
Headache	☐
Back Pain	☐
Chest Pain	☐
Heart Palpitations	☐
High Blood Pressure	☐
Lowered Immunity (colds)	☐
Upset Stomach	☐
Sleep Problems	☐
Anxiety	☐
Restlessness	☐

STRESS TATTLE-TALES

STRESS SYMPTOM	GOT IT?
Worrying	☐
Irritability	☐
Depressed or Sad	☐
Angry	☐
Insecure	☐
Can't Focus; Distracted	☐
Forgetful	☐
Feeling Burned Out	☐
Withdrawing from People	☐
Smoking or Drinking (More)	☐
Crying Spells	☐
Relationship Issues	☐
Change in Eating	☐

WEIGH THE DAY

PROS	CONS

WEIGH THE DAY

PROS	CONS

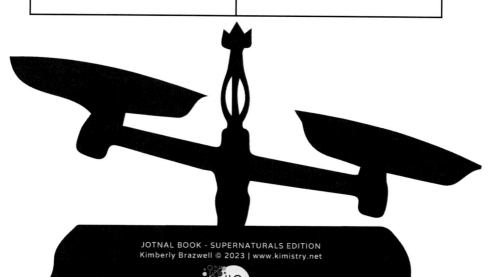

MOOD JOURNALING

One of the seemingly simplest questions a person is asked is, "How are you?" But the honest answer isn't that simple, is it? How do you typically answer this question? Do you tell the truth? Do you have a standard reply to this check-in? Do you believe people really want to know the answer to their question when you are asked?

Assume, in the Jotnal, that you are being asked, "How are you?" by someone who truly seeks to know and understand not only what you are feeling but why you feel the way you feel and how they can support you. The pages ahead will give you three different moods to feel and think through. Light days could be considered as "good moods". Meh days might be thought of as "okay or mediocre moods". Finally, shadow days are what we most often call "bad days". So... How are are? Use the pages ahead to share your thoughts and feelings about your moods.

MOOD INDEX REMINDER

SYMBOL	MOOD	ENERGETIC VIBE
	FAIRY	"I feel empty but I look beautiful."
	IMP	"I feel mischievous and energetic."
	SHAPESHIFTER	"I feel uncomfortable unless I change to match others."
	INDIGO	"I feel everyone and everything."
	WITCH	"I feel powerful in my connection to the elements."
	GHOST	"I feel invisible to most people."
	VAMPIRE	"I feel lifeless unless I feed off the energy of others."
	ZOMBIE	"I feel stuck between being alive and lifeless."

JOTNAL BOOK - SUPERNATURALS EDITION
Kimberly Brazwell © 2023 | www.kimistry.net

LIGHT DAY JOURNALING

DATE _____

ONE THING I WANT TO REMEMBER ABOUT TODAY
_____
_____
_____
_____
_____

TODAY I FELT...
_____
_____
_____
_____
_____

ONE THING THAT HELPED WAS...
_____
_____
_____
_____
_____

JOTNAL BOOK - SUPERNATURALS EDITION
Kimberly Brazwell © 2023 | www.kimistry.net

LIGHT DAY JOURNALING

DATE _____

ONE THING I WANT TO REMEMBER ABOUT TODAY

_____

_____

_____

_____

_____

TODAY I FELT...

_____

_____

_____

_____

_____

ONE THING THAT HELPED WAS...

_____

_____

_____

_____

_____

JOTNAL BOOK - SUPERNATURALS EDITION
Kimberly Brazwell © 2023 | www.kimistry.net

LIGHT DAY
JOURNALING

DATE _____

ONE THING I WANT TO REMEMBER ABOUT TODAY

_____

_____

_____

_____

_____

TODAY I FELT...

_____

_____

_____

_____

ONE THING THAT HELPED WAS...

_____

_____

_____

_____

_____

JOTNAL BOOK - SUPERNATURALS EDITION
Kimberly Brazwell © 2023 | www.kimistry.net

46

LIGHT DAY
JOURNALING

DATE _____

ONE THING I WANT TO REMEMBER ABOUT TODAY

_____

_____

_____

_____

_____

TODAY I FELT...

_____

_____

_____

_____

_____

ONE THING THAT HELPED WAS...

_____

_____

_____

_____

_____

_____

JOTNAL BOOK - SUPERNATURALS EDITION
Kimberly Brazwell © 2023 | www.kimistry.net

LIGHT DAY
JOURNALING

DATE _____

ONE THING I WANT TO REMEMBER ABOUT TODAY

_____

_____

_____

_____

_____

TODAY I FELT...

_____

_____

_____

_____

_____

ONE THING THAT HELPED WAS...

_____

_____

_____

_____

_____

JOTNAL BOOK - SUPERNATURALS EDITION
Kimberly Brazwell © 2023 | www.kimistry.net

48

MOOD INDEX REMINDER

SYMBOL	MOOD	ENERGETIC VIBE
	FAIRY	"I feel empty but I look beautiful."
	IMP	"I feel mischievous and energetic."
	SHAPESHIFTER	"I feel uncomfortable unless I change to match others."
	INDIGO	"I feel everyone and everything."
	WITCH	"I feel powerful in my connection to the elements."
	GHOST	"I feel invisible to most people."
	VAMPIRE	"I feel lifeless unless I feed off the energy of others."
	ZOMBIE	"I feel stuck between being alive and lifeless."

JOTNAL BOOK - SUPERNATURALS EDITION
Kimberly Brazwell © 2023 | www.kimistry.net

MEH DAY JOURNALING

DATE _____

ONE THING I SHOULD REMEMBER ABOUT TODAY

_____

_____

_____

_____

_____

TODAY I FELT...

_____

_____

_____

_____

_____

ONE THING THAT HELPED WAS...

_____

_____

_____

_____

_____

JOTNAL BOOK - SUPERNATURALS EDITION
Kimberly Brazwell © 2023 | www.kimistry.net

MEH DAY JOURNALING

DATE _____

ONE THING I SHOULD REMEMBER ABOUT TODAY

_____

_____

_____

_____

_____

TODAY I FELT...

_____

_____

_____

_____

ONE THING THAT HELPED WAS...

_____

_____

_____

_____

_____

JOTNAL BOOK - SUPERNATURALS EDITION
Kimberly Brazwell © 2023 | www.kimistry.net

MEH DAY JOURNALING

DATE _____

ONE THING I SHOULD REMEMBER ABOUT TODAY

_____

_____

_____

_____

_____

TODAY I FELT...

_____

_____

_____

_____

_____

ONE THING THAT HELPED WAS...

_____

_____

_____

_____

_____

JOTNAL BOOK - SUPERNATURALS EDITION
Kimberly Brazwell © 2023 | www.kimistry.net

MEH DAY
JOURNALING

DATE _____

ONE THING I SHOULD REMEMBER ABOUT TODAY

_____

_____

_____

_____

_____

TODAY I FELT...

_____

_____

_____

_____

_____

ONE THING THAT HELPED WAS...

_____

_____

_____

_____

_____

JOTNAL BOOK - SUPERNATURALS EDITION
Kimberly Brazwell © 2023 | www.kimistry.net

MEH DAY JOURNALING

DATE _____

ONE THING I SHOULD REMEMBER ABOUT TODAY

_____

_____

_____

_____

_____

TODAY I FELT...

_____

_____

_____

_____

_____

ONE THING THAT HELPED WAS...

_____

_____

_____

_____

_____

JOTNAL BOOK - SUPERNATURALS EDITION
Kimberly Brazwell © 2023 | www.kimistry.net

MOOD INDEX REMINDER

SYMBOL	MOOD	ENERGETIC VIBE
	FAIRY	"I feel empty but I look beautiful."
	IMP	"I feel mischievous and energetic."
	SHAPESHIFTER	"I feel uncomfortable unless I change to match others."
	INDIGO	"I feel everyone and everything."
	WITCH	"I feel powerful in my connection to the elements."
	GHOST	"I feel invisible to most people."
	VAMPIRE	"I feel lifeless unless I feed off the energy of others."
	ZOMBIE	"I feel stuck between being alive and lifeless."

JOTNAL BOOK - SUPERNATURALS EDITION
Kimberly Brazwell © 2023 | www.kimistry.net

SHADOW DAY JOURNALING

DATE

ONE THING I NEED TO REMEMBER ABOUT TODAY

TODAY I FELT...

ONE THING THAT HELPED WAS...

SHADOW DAY JOURNALING

DATE _____

ONE THING I NEED TO REMEMBER ABOUT TODAY

_____

_____

_____

_____

_____

_____

TODAY I FELT...

_____

_____

_____

_____

_____

ONE THING THAT HELPED WAS...

_____

_____

_____

_____

_____

_____

JOTNAL BOOK - SUPERNATURALS EDITION
Kimberly Brazwell © 2023 | www.kimistry.net

SHADOW DAY
JOURNALING

DATE _____

ONE THING I NEED TO REMEMBER ABOUT TODAY

_____
_____
_____
_____
_____

TODAY I FELT...

_____
_____
_____
_____
_____

ONE THING THAT HELPED WAS...

_____
_____
_____
_____
_____

SHADOW DAY JOURNALING

DATE _____

ONE THING I NEED TO REMEMBER ABOUT TODAY

_____

_____

_____

_____

_____

TODAY I FELT...

_____

_____

_____

_____

_____

ONE THING THAT HELPED WAS...

_____

_____

_____

_____

_____

SHADOW DAY JOURNALING

DATE _____

ONE THING I NEED TO REMEMBER ABOUT TODAY

_____

_____

_____

_____

_____

TODAY I FELT...

_____

_____

_____

_____

ONE THING THAT HELPED WAS...

_____

_____

_____

_____

_____

JOTNAL BOOK - SUPERNATURALS EDITION
Kimberly Brazwell © 2023 | www.kimistry.net

FOOD JOURNALING

Did you think this portion of the Jotnal was a place to judge your weight, physical appearance and eating habits? Guess again! Let's think about food and healing in a different way. Stress, trauma, overstimulation, depression, anxiety and burnout often have physiological manifestations. In other words, how we feel emotionally can impact our physical health, causing complications as well as behavioral issues and relationship drama.

Have you ever said things like, "I have a gut feeling?" Has an unpleasant situation ever made you, "Sick to your stomach?" These statements are true because emotions show up in your gastrointestinal system. Heartburn. Nausea. Indigestion. Constipation. Diarrhea. And more. What we do or don't eat, when we do or don't eat and why we do or don't eat has so much more to do with our spirits than our waist line. Track your eating in comparison to your healing journey and see what you discover!

DATE _____

WHAT WAS ON THE MENU THIS WEEK?

M	
T	
W	
T	
F	
S	
S	

DATE _____

WHAT WAS ON THE MENU THIS WEEK?

M	
T	
W	
T	
F	
S	
S	

DATE _____

WHAT WAS ON THE MENU THIS WEEK?

M	
T	
W	
T	
F	
S	
S	

DATE _____

WHAT WAS ON THE MENU THIS WEEK?

M
T
W
T
F
S
S

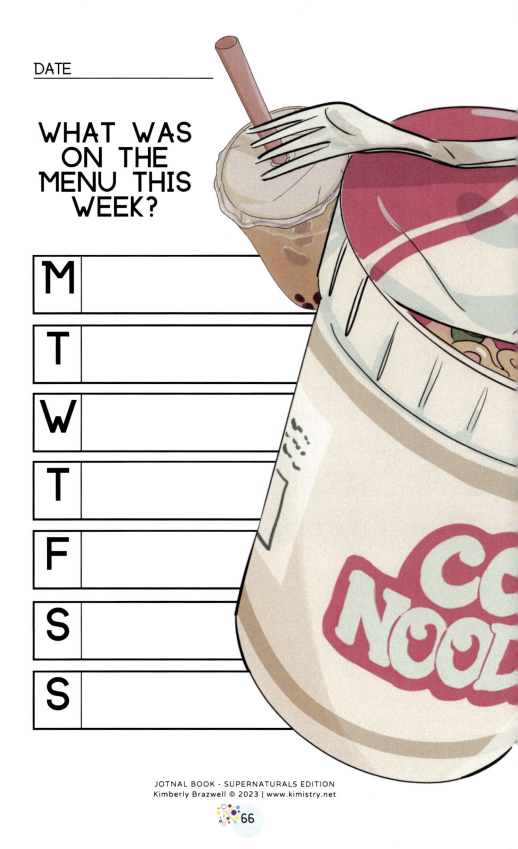

SUMMARY STORIES

Let's be honest. There are going to be days during your Jotnal use when you don't have the time, energy, capacity or desire to do deep reflection and writing. You might miss several days in a row of logging your thoughts and feelings. Luckily, we thought of that, too.

The next section will give you space and permission to go back and reflect if and when you can't sit still in the moment. Use the start or end of the week to think back on what did and didn't work for you. Carve out a few minutes at the beginning of your day to think about yesterday. Or perhaps it might be easier to wait until the end of your day to think about the most recent 24 hours. No matter what, give yourself the gift of time and stillness to let silence be a voice. In the silence of your mind, might you be able to gather your thoughts and summarize what you are noticing on your journey?

REFLECTION & RECAP

DATE _____

ON AVERAGE LAST WEEK, I FELT:

AWESOME   GOOD   OKAY   NOT GOOD   HORRIBLE

WHY DO I THINK I FELT HOW I FELT?
_____
_____
_____
_____

WHAT (AND/OR WHO) DID I NEED?
_____
_____
_____
_____

HOW WILL I BE GOOD TO MYSELF THIS WEEK?
_____

REFLECTION & RECAP

DATE _____

ON AVERAGE LAST WEEK, I FELT:

AWESOME   GOOD   OKAY   NOT GOOD   HORRIBLE

WHY DO I THINK I FELT HOW I FELT?
_____
_____
_____
_____

WHAT (AND/OR WHO) DID I NEED?
_____
_____
_____
_____

HOW WILL I BE GOOD TO MYSELF THIS WEEK?
_____

REFLECTION & RECAP

DATE _____

ON AVERAGE LAST WEEK, I FELT:

AWESOME   GOOD   OKAY   NOT GOOD   HORRIBLE

WHY DO I THINK I FELT HOW I FELT?

_____
_____
_____
_____

WHAT (AND/OR WHO) DID I NEED?

_____
_____
_____
_____

HOW WILL I BE GOOD TO MYSELF THIS WEEK?

_____

REFLECTION & RECAP

DATE _____

ON AVERAGE LAST WEEK, I FELT:

AWESOME   GOOD   OKAY   NOT GOOD   HORRIBLE

WHY DO I THINK I FELT HOW I FELT?

_____
_____
_____
_____

WHAT (AND/OR WHO) DID I NEED?

_____
_____
_____
_____

HOW WILL I BE GOOD TO MYSELF THIS WEEK?

_____

JOTNAL BOOK - SUPERNATURALS EDITION
Kimberly Brazwell © 2023 | www.kimistry.net

REFLECTION & RECAP

DATE _____

ON AVERAGE LAST WEEK, I FELT:

AWESOME   GOOD   OKAY   NOT GOOD   HORRIBLE

WHY DO I THINK I FELT HOW I FELT?

_____
_____
_____

WHAT (AND/OR WHO) DID I NEED?

_____
_____
_____

HOW WILL I BE GOOD TO MYSELF THIS WEEK?

_____

QUICK CHECK-IN

DATE _____

I WOKE UP FEELING:

HOW THE DAY STARTED:

HOW IT'S GOING RIGHT NOW:

HOW IT'S GOING RIGHT NOW:

MY FINAL RATING FOR TODAY:
☆ ☆ ☆ ☆ ☆

MY #1 PLAN FOR TOMORROW:

QUICK CHECK-IN

DATE _____

I WOKE UP FEELING:

HOW THE DAY STARTED:

HOW IT'S GOING RIGHT NOW:

HOW IT'S GOING RIGHT NOW:

MY FINAL RATING FOR TODAY:

MY #1 PLAN FOR TOMORROW:

JOTNAL BOOK - SUPERNATURALS EDITION
Kimberly Brazwell © 2023 | www.kimistry.net

QUICK CHECK-IN

DATE _____

I WOKE UP FEELING:

HOW THE DAY STARTED:

HOW IT'S GOING RIGHT NOW:

HOW IT'S GOING RIGHT NOW:

MY FINAL RATING FOR TODAY:

MY #1 PLAN FOR TOMORROW:

JOTNAL BOOK - SUPERNATURALS EDITION
Kimberly Brazwell © 2023 | www.kimistry.net

QUICK CHECK-IN

DATE _____

I WOKE UP FEELING:

HOW THE DAY STARTED:

HOW IT'S GOING RIGHT NOW:

HOW IT'S GOING RIGHT NOW:

MY FINAL RATING FOR TODAY:
☆ ☆ ☆ ☆ ☆

MY #1 PLAN FOR TOMORROW:

QUICK CHECK-IN

DATE _____

I WOKE UP FEELING:

HOW THE DAY STARTED:

HOW IT'S GOING RIGHT NOW:

HOW IT'S GOING RIGHT NOW:

MY FINAL RATING FOR TODAY:
☆ ☆ ☆ ☆

MY #1 PLAN FOR TOMORROW:

JOTNAL BOOK - SUPERNATURALS EDITION
Kimberly Brazwell © 2023 | www.kimistry.net

80

FREE WRITING

Can we just take a second and celebrate?! You are nearing the end of this Jotnal experience. Look at how much you've processed. You've responded to pulse checks, check-ins, list-making, brief writing prompts, and many other activities and exercises to get an idea of what you are thinking, feeling and experiencing on a deeper level. Now it's time to let loose and be boundless in what your head and heart want to express!

This next section is a space you can use anytime you want - to write whatever you want. One tip or suggestion for this section might be to use the additional space to further process an idea or prompt given to you earlier in the Jotnal. Perhaps your mind is stimulated and you need to flesh out some ideas. The next pages are prompt and question-free. Use your voice and tell your story uncensored and unfiltered.

I-PAGE JOURNALING

DATE _____

_____

_____

_____

_____

_____

_____

_____

_____

_____

_____

_____

_____

_____

_____

_____

_____

_____

_____

_____

_____

_____

_____

_____

JOTNAL BOOK - SUPERNATURALS EDITION
Kimberly Brazwell © 2023 | www.kimistry.net

I-PAGE JOURNALING

DATE _____

_____

_____

_____

_____

_____

_____

_____

_____

_____

_____

_____

_____

_____

_____

_____

_____

_____

_____

_____

_____

_____

_____

1-PAGE JOURNALING

DATE _____

_____

_____

_____

_____

_____

_____

_____

_____

_____

_____

_____

_____

_____

_____

_____

_____

_____

_____

_____

_____

_____

_____

_____

_____

I-PAGE JOURNALING

DATE _____

_____

_____

_____

_____

_____

_____

_____

_____

_____

_____

_____

_____

_____

_____

_____

_____

_____

_____

_____

_____

_____

_____

1-PAGE JOURNALING

DATE _____

_____
_____
_____
_____
_____
_____
_____
_____
_____
_____
_____
_____
_____
_____
_____
_____
_____
_____
_____
_____
_____
_____

1-PAGE JOURNALING

DATE _____

_____

_____

_____

_____

_____

_____

_____

_____

_____

_____

_____

_____

_____

_____

_____

_____

_____

_____

_____

_____

_____

_____

_____

_____

DOODLES

Sometimes paragraphs, sentences and big words can't quite capture what you want and need to say. Do you think in pictures? Do ideas and thoughts come to you in images and abstract lists? You might be a person whose brain gravitates toward mind-mapping.

Think of mind-mapping as brain storming with pictures, scribbles, doodles and minimal words or phrases. If illustrating your idea might help you think things through, especially before you write down your thoughts in more detail, this area of the Jotnal might be a cool practice and ideating space for you.

MIND-MAPPING EXAMPLE
This mind map was an exploration of how the creator was feeling. They realized they sometimes don't feel anything at all. Other times, they feel separate from other people and like a stranger in their own body. When they couldn't find the words to capture all they were feeling, it made more sense to draw out the emotions rather than to write and explain them.

FIGHTING FOR ME

One unique thing to remember about supernatural moods is that they give you access to something special and powerful inside. Even when you're not at your best, you always have access to that special something.

Do you feel that small burning sensation? This time, what if it's not indigestion or heartburn? What if it's the fire in your belly? If this Jotnal has caused you to experience any kind of GOOD discomfort, consider that the invitation for you to start fighting for YOU! You are your first revolution. You are worthy. You have value. You deserve love, care, safety and compassion.

The final section of the Jotnal includes exercises and activities to help you reflect on how to ask for - and demand - what you want and need. Use this section to tap into your power. It never left you; it's been here the whole time, waiting to be rediscovered and reclaimed. Now is YOUR time to rise, superhuman!

"Everyone keeps telling me how my story is supposed to go. Sorry, I'm doing my own thing."

MILES MORALES, SPIDER-MAN.
ARTIST. VIGILANTE. ANOMOLY.

HOW OFTEN DO YOU CODESWITCH?

Check the boxes below that resonate as true for you based on your job or school.

1. I don't change the type of music or the volume at which I listen to my music when I'm away from home or personal property (e.g. my car).
2. I use similar lexicon and phrasing regardless of who I am in conversation with.
3. I don't dress differently when I want to be taken seriously.
4. I feel comfortable being myself 1:1 or in group settings.
5. I am seldom ostracized or isolated for speaking up.
6. I am seldom "talked to" or disciplined for defending myself.
7. I don't speak differently when I want to be taken seriously.
8. I don't have to modify my behavior to avoid being stereotyped.
9. I often feel like I am around people who understand me.
10. I dress a certain way when I want to feel comfortable.
11. I'm typically not comfortable until I'm at home.
12. I am seldom asked to lower my voice by someone outside of my conversation group while talking.
13. My excitement or passion in conversation has never been mistaken for anger.
14. I have never avoided conversation topics for fear that I might be offended or upset.
15. I have no need to change pronouns or use generic descriptors when speaking about my romantic life in conversation.
16. I feel comfortable eating all kinds of foods in front of other people.
17. I am seldom labeled a troublemaker for telling the truth.
18. I don't know what it's like to laugh or shrug off offensive comments or behavior made about a group to which I belong.
19. I have never worried about my smell being offensive to others.
20. I introduce myself and get to know people the same way in all kinds of environments.
21. I am comfortable showing all aspects of my personality in front of people (e.g. humor).

JOTNAL BOOK - SUPERNATURALS EDITION
Kimberly Brazwell © 2023 | www.kimistry.net

CODESWITCH CHECKLIST CONT.'D

22. I feel comfortable showing my creative talents in front of others.

23. I feel comfortable asking questions in groups of people.

24. I am comfortable adding commentary in group conversation.

25. I never second-guess things I say in conversation.

26. I rarely feel like I'm talking too much.

27. I am pretty confident that people can relate to my stories and experiences.

28. When I share my stories and experience, listeners usually affirm my story with questions or comments as opposed to awkward silence.

29. I typically don't overthink about how I'm being perceived.

30. I rarely shut down in conversations.

31. I rarely feel the need to have an attitude or edge to protect myself.

32. I rarely feel like I'm asking a stupid question.

33. I typically feel affirmed and rewarded for speaking up.

34. Having an opinion that's different from other people in a conversation doesn't make me feel like I need to defend myself.

35. I have never been told to calm down when expressing my opinion on something.

36. I have never been advised to be less expressive.

37. I don't expect any negative consequences if I speak my mind.

38. I don't feel like I have to be perfect in order to be perceived as successful or smart.

39. I have never directly been called passive or aggressive.

40. I have friends at school or work who "get me".

41. I am often complimented for being "articulate".

42. I see images at school or work of people who look like me all the time.

43. I don't feel like parts of my identity are made to be invisible.

44. I never have been over-talked in conversations.

45. I have never been accused of being wrong or been given advise when sharing a story or experience.

JOTNAL BOOK - SUPERNATURALS EDITION
Kimberly Brazwell © 2023 | www.kimistry.net

CODESWITCH CHECKLIST CONT.'D

☐	46. I have never been corrected about my feelings or told what to feel when sharing a story or experience.
☐	47. I have never felt pitied after sharing a story or experience.
☐	48. I seldom feel talked down to by others.
☐	49. I have never had anyone suggest that I *need* to be mentored.
☐	50. I rarely feel minimized or common after sharing a story or experience.
☐	51. I am seldom told, "You're not the only one..." after sharing a story or experience.
☐	52. I am often told, "Good idea!" when I offer a suggestion or opinion.
☐	53. I am often told, "We can try it" when I offer a suggestion or opinion.
☐	54. It has never been stated or implied that I should, "Stay in my lane".
☐	55. I am seldom "talked to" or disciplined for telling the truth.
☐	56. I have seldom entered a space where I am the only person of my ethnic or gender identity.
☐	57. I have people at work or school who I trust completely.

FIT PRIVILEGE CHECKLIST SCORING

Fit privilege gives a framework for understanding how "safe", comfortable or non-threatening a space feels and how authentic you feel in said space.
How much fit privilege do you perceive to have? Please circle one.

Range of Items Checked	Degree of Codeswitching
0-12 items checked	CONSIDERABLE CODESWITCHING
13-30 items checked	MODERATE CODESWITCHING
31+ items checked	MINIMAL CODESWITCHING

FAMILY MANIFESTO

NEVER FORGET YOUR SUPERNATURAL FAMILY!

Our "family" can change from biological relationships to people with whom we <u>choose</u> to be in relationship. Use this fill-in-the-blank form to remember who matters to you and how you fight for your <u>chosen</u> family!

When I hear the song

1. [   ]
ENCOURAGING / FIGHT SONG

it reminds me of

2. [   ]
NAME OF ELDER FAMILY MEMBER(S)

and how they fought through

3. [   ]
THE ELDER'S WELLNESS BARRIER

to make sure our lives would be better. Because of them, I better understand

4. [   ]
EMPATHY LESSON

And although I recognize my family's fight with

5. [   ]
FAMILY WELLNESS BARRIER(S)

JOTNAL BOOK - SUPERNATURALS EDITION
Kimberly Brazwell © 2023 | www.kimistry.net

FAMILY MANIFESTO, CONT.'D.

I won't use

6. _____

INSTITUTIONAL BARRIER(S)

as an excuse to allow my family
to be disengaged. I know who I am
and I remember who we are.
My commitment is to ensure my loved ones

7. _____

DESIRED FAMILY LEGACY I WANT TO UPHOLD

So, I commit to stay present by

8. _____

HOW I FIGHT FOR LEGACY

because

9. _____

NAME OF FAMILY ELDER(S)

did the heavy lifting and I will
continue the legacy!

JOTNAL BOOK - SUPERNATURALS EDITION
Kimberly Brazwell © 2023 | www.kimistry.net

SELF-ADVOCACY MANIFESTO

NOW MAKE A DECLARATION TO FIGHT FOR YOU!

Use this fill-in-the-blank form to write yourself a commitment to prioritize your self care, your needs and your value. You're worth fighting for!

When I hear the song

1. ☐
   ENCOURAGING / FIGHT SONG

it reminds me of my

2. ☐
   SUPERNATURAL MOOD I OFTEN EXPERIENCE

and how challenges with

3. ☐
   WELLNESS BARRIER(S) AT THAT TIME

got the best of me at some point. But I'm better prepared to ask for

4. ☐
   WHAT YOU NEEDED IN THAT MOMENT

because I remember how I fought through issues with

5. ☐
   ANOTHER CHALLENGING WELLNESS BARRIER

JOTNAL BOOK - SUPERNATURALS EDITION
Kimberly Brazwell © 2023 | www.kimistry.net

SELF-ADVOCACY MANIFESTO, CONT.'D

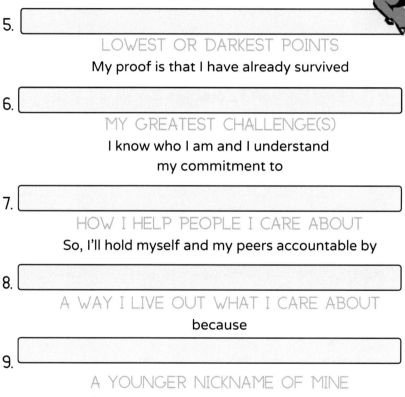

I <u>know</u> I can push through when my fears make me feel like I

5. ☐

LOWEST OR DARKEST POINTS

My proof is that I have already survived

6. ☐

MY GREATEST CHALLENGE(S)

I know who I am and I understand my commitment to

7. ☐

HOW I HELP PEOPLE I CARE ABOUT

So, I'll hold myself and my peers accountable by

8. ☐

A WAY I LIVE OUT WHAT I CARE ABOUT

because

9. ☐

A YOUNGER NICKNAME OF MINE

needs/needed me to never stop fighting for myself!

4-5-6 TALK TABLE

HOW DO YOU DEAL WITH CONFLICT AND "DYNAMIC TENSION"?

What happens when the internal tension grows to be too much to bear? It's time to speak up and use your voice! The 4-5-6 Talk Table provides steps on practical suggestions for working through tense moments when your identity, power and privileges are in play.

"4 • 5 • 6" Dynamic Tension Talk Table

Practical Suggestions for Working through Tense Moments When Implicit Bias, Identity and/or Privilege Are in Play

FIRST THINGS FIRST	WHEN OUCH HAPPENS	AFTER THE CONVERSATION
1. Seek Experiences to Break Your Stereotypes. Don't walk away or shut down; engage in conversation about the topic you don't know, don't understand, or don't like.	**1. Notice and Name the Pain.** When something is said or experienced that feels harsh, hurtful or offensive to you, actually say "ouch" out loud.	**1. My People vs. My Own Person** It's okay to take a timeout and seek comfort from the people who know and understand your pain. Just remind others that you are your own person and cannot speak for all of your people.
2. Set Your Rules for Engagement. Clearly state what your needs are and what your deal breakers are in order to keep talking and/or stay in the moment.	**2. Tell the "Ouch" Story.** Tell a/the story you have experienced or are experiencing that involves you feeling hurt.	**2. Check In to See How You Can Help.** If you think that someone may be hurt or offended by something (and you're pretty sure you didn't do it), confidentially ask her/him: *"Are you okay? How can I help?"*
3. Notice Facts vs. Feelings. Express what it is about this topic that makes you feel disconnected. And try to articulate your truth behind why you're upset.	**3. Pay the "Ouch" Forward.** Have someone retell your story as s/he heard it and with words that show what s/he noticed about how you might feel about your story.	**3. Be Kind without Keeping Score.** Do the right thing without waiting for gratitude, an apology, etc. in return.
4. Be Curious When You Don't "Get" It. If during conversation, you feel yourself missing the point, ask that it be broken down for you in smaller pieces so you can better understand.	**4. Don't Talk; Just Listen.** If it gets uncomfortable and the discomfort (which could be silence) becomes painful, stop debating. Acknowledge the "ouch", sit there, and let silence be a voice. If desired, the "ouch" can be explained later.	**4. Show Compassion.** Find something about your 'opponent' to compliment that s/he wouldn't expect you to notice or affirm. Then affirm it out loud.
	5. Say Sorry …And Mean It. Ultimately, if *you* have caused or did nothing to prevent the "ouch", apologize for your part in causing someone pain.	**5. Practice Feeling Uncomfortable.** Try a new activity or social circle that doesn't play to your strengths. Notice how you feel and how you're treated when you are not winning or leading.
		6. Be Brave and Bold When You Know You Can't Be Hurt. Use your privilege for *good* and tell the truth to and/or about those who also share your privilege. Be honest and speak up when power is being abused.

JOTNAL BOOK - SUPERNATURALS EDITION
Kimberly Brazwell © 2023 | www.kimistry.net

4-5-6 TALK TABLE ACTIVITY, PT. 1

FIRST THINGS FIRST

1. SEEK EXPERIENCES TO BREAK YOUR STEREOTYPES.
What is a stereotype I have and what kind of experience will help me break it?

2. SET YOUR RULES FOR ENGAGEMENT.
What conditions and agreements would help me talk through this issue?

3. NOTICE FACTS VS. FEELINGS.
What facts to I notice and what feelings am I experiencing?

4. BE CURIOUS WHEN YOU DON'T "GET" IT.
What is it I feel I am not understanding? What doesn't make sense or is unclear?

4-5-6 TALK TABLE ACTIVITY, PT. 2

WHEN OUCH HAPPENS

1. NOTICE AND NAME THE PAIN.
Ouch! What is it that's hurting me or making me feel uncomfortable?

2. TELL THE "OUCH" STORY.
How might I explain exactly what the situation was that led to my pain?

3. PAY THE "OUCH" FORWARD.
What did the person who is listening to my story hear me say?

4. DON'T TALK; JUST LISTEN.
Is it possible that I have caused pain to someone else?

5. SAY SORRY ...AND MEAN IT.
If I have offended someone, am I willing to apologize and change my behavior?

JOTNAL BOOK - SUPERNATURALS EDITION
Kimberly Brazwell © 2023 | www.kimistry.net

4-5-6 TALK TABLE ACTIVITY, PT. 3

AFTER THE CONVERSATION

1. MY PEOPLE VS. MY OWN PERSON
What part of my identity is hurting and will private time with people from this identity group will bring me comfort?

2. CHECK IN TO SEE HOW YOU CAN HELP.
Who can I support in this moment and what do they need?

3. BE KIND WITHOUT KEEPING SCORE.
What good thing can I do for someone without expecting something in return?

4. SHOW COMPASSION.
Can I identify something good in my antagonist and am I willing to affirm them?

5. PRACTICE FEELING UNCOMFORTABLE.
What uncomfortable thing can or will I do to that will help me grow?

6. BE BRAVE AND BOLD WHEN YOU KNOW YOU CAN'T BE HURT.
How or where do I have power and how can I speak truth through this power?

JOTNAL BOOK - SUPERNATURALS EDITION
Kimberly Brazwell © 2023 | www.kimistry.net

DATE _____

DEAR JOTNAL,

HERE'S WHAT I'M LEARNING ABOUT MYSELF SO FAR...

_____

_____

_____

_____

_____

_____

_____

_____

_____

_____

_____

_____

_____

_____

_____

JOTNAL BOOK - SUPERNATURALS EDITION
Kimberly Brazwell © 2023 | www.kimistry.net

Made in the USA
Middletown, DE
02 July 2024